ANGEL TALK

ANGEL TALK

by **Ruth Crystal**

Foreword by
Reverend Stevan J. Thayer

Illustrations
Paul W. McCormack

Contributing Editor
Story Lucile Ducey

EDIN
BOOKS
Inc.

Edin Books, Inc.
P.O. Box 59
Gillette, New Jersey 07933
908-MIS-EDIN ◆ 908·647–3346

Cover design: Dunn+Associates, Hayward, WI
Editorial review: Linda Sue Nathanson, Ph.D., Paula Sirois and Allan Varian
Editor's Assistant: Victoria Anderson
Typesetting: Jim Richards

Printed in the United States of America
    1st printing   1/96   5,000
    2nd printing   8/96   5,000

Integrated Energy Therapy is a registered trademark of The Center of Being, Inc.

Publisher's Cataloging in Publication
    (Prepared by Quality Books Inc.)

Crystal, Ruth.
    Angel talk / by Ruth Crystal.
    p. cm.
    Preassigned LCCN: 95-61345.
    ISBN 1-887010-01-7.

    1. Angels--Miscellanea. 2. Spirit writings.   I. Title

BF1290.B36 1996   291.2'15
                                                      QB195-20595

This book is dedicated
from Angels
with love and devotion
to all the beings on this Earth.

This book is dedicated
from Ruthie
to my Mother Mary in heaven...

I miss you, sweet lady.

This book is written for those who read it.
If these pages have found their way into your hands,
there is a message here for you.

Take this book and place it beneath your pillow.
When the stars are bright and the moon is in the sky,
whisper it your prayers, your wishes, your heartfelt dreams.
Be surprised at what your spirit encounters.

Give this book to someone you love.
Give this book to someone who does not love you.

Send this book to a country you love.
Send this book to a country that does not love yours.

Send this book out to places far away.
Receive love back in many ways yet unknown.
Translate this book into many languages.
Receive peace back in all ways.

Contents

Illustrations   x

Foreword by Reverend Stevan J. Thayer   xi

Preface   xvi

Angel Talk Glossary   xix

1   Ruthie's Story   1

2   Angel Visions   15

3   Lessons on Poetic Existence   35

4   Your Personal Journey   47

5   Love Poetry & Universal Messages for all Beings   73

6   Angels Illuminate Love   90

7   Angel Towers   102

8   Earth Flowers   109

9   Angel Knowledge   116

10   Bedtime Stories for Big and Little People: 142
     Dreamy Angel Words for Ageless Beings

From Ruthie   164

Future Books   165

Illustrations

Angel Ariel   5, 20

Tiny Angel With Hummingbird Wings   3, 23

Angel Lady in the Silver Cage Dress   25

Piggyback Angel   27

Angel Flying in the Forest   29

Angels That Mind Our Precious Souls   33, back cover

Foreword

The pages of *Angel Talk* are filled with inspiring guidance, lovingly offered to all its readers through the person of Ruth Crystal. Quite unlike other books that are *about* angels, this one has been written *by* angels.

For Ruth, this has been a new phenomenon. Prior to the summer of 1994, Ruth had no interest in or awareness of angels. She was not looking to invoke angels; nevertheless, these beings of light began to appear to her. When Ruth first saw these images, as you may well imagine, she was both stunned and awestruck. She thought she must be hallucinating. Yet the angels kept appearing and, soon, she could no longer deny their existence. The angels made it clear to her: they were giving her messages "for all people." She recorded their visits and conversations, and so this book has come to be.

The angels' words are poetic, clear and direct. Their messages often have meanings on many levels and should not only be enjoyed as they are, but also pondered to find the deeper layers of significance in all areas of your life.

Angel Encounters

Angel encounters have been depicted throughout history in art, literature and the Bible. Testimonies to the angelic realm and its messengers are essential parts of the Kabala, the Bible's Old and New Testaments and the Koran. Winged guardians from the skies are also present in the early sacred writings and ancient art of the Indian, Sumerian, Egyptian and Greek civilizations. Winged beings who visit and inspire humankind are recorded in the spiritual traditions of the ancient Native American cultures as well. We can even find images of half-human, half-birdlike beings in the art of the Goddess-worshipping cultures that date back to 20,000 BC.

Today, newspapers, television, magazines and books are filled with people reporting sightings of, having conversations with, being touched and even being rescued by nonphysical life forms, seen by many as the angels of traditional religious teachings. There are a variety of theories as to who and what these entities are, and they have been given a multitude of names and ranks such as heavenly spirits, celestial beings, beings of light, winged messengers, seraphim, cherubim, angels, archangels and the Great Spirits of the Six Directions.

While our understanding of angels varies among different belief systems, the experiences that people have during angelic encounters are always similar—feelings of love, peace of mind, support and guidance. Beyond the comfort one gains from such other-worldly exchanges, encounters with angels can provide us with a deep spiritual knowing that can completely transform our lives.

The Spiritual Journey

Life is a journey of personal healing and spiritual development. Every event, situation and experience in one's life is an integral part of this journey. Our purpose on this path is to recognize our spiritual nature and to bring forth our full potential so that we evolve spiritually.

We come to recognize our spiritual nature when we see ourselves, not defined or limited by our physical bodies, but as interconnected to and interdependent with all of life and what has been called: God, Goddess, Great Spirit, Atman, Allah, the Tao and Universal Mind. As we explore our inner selves, we can come to know that there is a part of us that lives beyond the death of the physical body. We can learn to actively work with this aspect of our mind to expand our conscious awareness. Spiritual evolution is a process of unfolding. Extrasensory experiences, such as Ruth has, are a natural outgrowth of this process.

Ways to Experience Angels

The three extrasensory, intuitive ways we can experience angels and other levels of the spiritual realm are called clairsentience, clairvoyance and clairaudience. *Clairsentience* refers to extrasensory abilities that enable one to *feel* the loving, gentle presence of angels. While actual physical sensations vary, a fairly common experience is to feel an inrush of warmth accompanied by feelings of love, peace, equanimity, tranquillity and joy. *Clairvoyance* refers to extrasensory visual abilities that allow one to *see* angels. There are two general kinds of clairvoyant experiences. The first involves seeing with the inner eye; images form in the mind's eye while the eyes are closed. The other involves seeing the images with eyes open. *Clairaudience* refers to extrasensory abilities involving internal or external *hearing*. With external clairaudience, it is possible to actually receive messages that appear to emanate from an unseen source such as in hearing an angel speak to you. With internal clairaudience, the words form in your mind, which you can then either write down or say out loud. They may even feel like your own thoughts, but with angelic communication, you may find the words forming faster than your conscious mind can create them.

Ruth sees the extraordinary, detailed images of peaceful angelic beings that are wonderfully illustrated in this book, and she receives angelic messages both internally, through an inner voice, and externally, from what seems like the air around her. She sometimes has to write quickly to capture the entire message. When this happens, it is only after the message has stopped that she can read and comprehend it, often consulting a dictionary for unfamiliar words.

While many people have no awareness of extrasensory capabilities, such gifts can often be developed. Ruth helps people connect with their angels as part of her angel workshops (See "From Ruthie," page 165.)

Path to Publishing

Early on, the angel's guidance was for Ruth alone. When people heard of her experiences, they sought her out for their own angelic guidance. The angels encouraged Ruth to share their messages and poetry with everyone. Angel Ariel told her the words she was receiving were important, that they would be published and bring the angel messages to the world. She questioned how she would find a publisher. Ariel assured her that all was being taken care of. And so, she continued to carefully record each message, resulting in this delightful, inspirational book of *Angel Talk.*

Reverend Stevan J. Thayer
Interfaith Minister & Spiritual Director
The Center of Being, Inc.
Holmdel, NJ

# Preface

I was upset. I was nerve-wracked. I was afraid to go one way, frightened of the other. I feared. There seemed to be nowhere for me to go. I was searching for shelter from my severely shattered emotional state brought on by the hurts and heartaches of every-day life.

I prayed. I prayed as I suffered in fear. I began to pray in ways I had never before expressed. I prayed for people I did not like. I prayed for people who had no use for me. I prayed for people who would not pray for me. I prayed for foreign countries threatening the United States. I prayed for perpetration to end. I prayed for the souls of criminals. I prayed for hatred to stop.

For one small moment, I sensed I was not alone and looked up. An angel with wings from ceiling to floor and eyes like halogen lights gazed at me. It was like:

- The New York skyline lit up after The Blackout.

- New Year's Eve at Times Square on this planet and all others in the universe.

- Easter and a zillion baby chicks hatched from eggs.

- Chinese New Year and every fortune cookie read:

"COME AND GET YOUR LOVE, RUTHIE!"

Why did I write this book?
Angels told me the words. I merely put them on paper.

Who should read this book?
Anyone interested in the words of angels. Anyone experiencing that longing to know, truly, that there is more love available than we on Earth ever realized, until now.

What is offered in this book?
In these pages there is an immense offering of love, attention and wisdom by universal winged beings of light and ecstasy.

Why do angels fly?
Because they deserve to fly.

In terms of happiness, in terms of joy, in terms of sadness, in terms of despair, these writings can offer soaring elation or comforting solace for a hungry soul.

In times of anxiety, in times of fear, in times of true connection with nature, in times of prayer, angels have come to me, shown themselves and given me the words to find myself.

In each instance, angels asked for their words to be passed on to more people — so we on Earth may share.

Where there was once silence,
Where there was once unoccupied space,
Where there was once no one to answer,
Where there was once no light to turn on,
There is now an Angel.

Angel Ariel

The angels have communicated to me in many places, in many ways and whispered all these words into my heart. They long for many people, hopefully all people, to know just how much love and knowledge they deliver to earth from God. It is within these pages that words of angels are offered to everyone as a spiritual gift.

Thank you loving, wise angels for all you have given me.

If Angels walk among us,
And guide us through our day,
They can visit our most secret dreams,
And carry us away.

Angel Ariel

Angel Talk Glossary

Written by Ruthie with Angels
(longing to connect with us)

All Ways	Every physical direction possible in the universe. In angel terms, time is nonexistent, so all ways may also be defined as forever and eternal.
Awareness	A being's unlimited power to expand and connect on the way to enlightenment.
Beauty	The inherent quality in all sentient beings to be admired and loved for merely existing.
Capable	Owning the free will to experience God, angels, love.
Creation	Where God and angels be.
Earth-being	Any live being on Earth (this planet) capable of experiencing feelings, sensations and emotions.
Earth-turns	The rotation of our planet which delivers each new day. Time is non-existent to angels so Earth-turns are angel words for our Earth days.
Enlightenment	That wonderful space of our universe where your soul meets creation.
Ethers	The dimension (space) in the universe where angels dwell.

Free Will	The angels' job is to watch, nurture, protect what God has them tend...which is us. Angels have the power to guide us if we pray and invite them with our free will. These winged beings will help us keep our path clear on the way to enlightenment. They also keep us safe as we search for that path. If we invite an angel, ask for guidance from an angel, pray for the attention of an angel, our journey through this life shall be surrounded with love. Your free will has the ability to invite all the love in creation. As you read this, angels are patiently waiting for their invitation to love you.
God-love	The total emotion of pure attention delivered by angels from God.
God	The higher being to which a soul prays. That which a soul regards as the "maker."
Heaven	That place (destination) where each soul meets God and where angels are created. The archaic spelling, "heavan" is the angels' preference.
Journey	The passage each soul embarks upon to follow its path to enlightenment.
Love	In angelic terms, this definition constantly expands as our awareness of beauty and God evolves.
Mind-view	A limited space in your perception.
Path	Each soul owns a destiny through its life to meet God. Angels refer to this destiny as our path.

Realm   A domain of power. One of many domains in the
                 universe. There be an Earth realm, angel realm
                 and realms yet to be discovered by us!
Self   A sentient being aware of his consciousness and
                 emotions.
Sentient being   Any live being in the universe capable of experi-
                 encing feeling, sensations and emotions.
Soul-shine   That love we create within ourselves to share with
                 each other. As we fill another being with love and
                 beauty, soul-shine is the result.

Editor's note:

Out of respect for what Ruthie tells us are the angels' wishes, we are
including archaic forms of language (i.e. "all ways" instead of "always," "be"
instead of "is," "mankind" instead of "humankind") and hyphenated words
created by the angels when there was no equivalent word available in our
language (i.e. soul-shine, mind-view, God-warmth, mind-picture).

CHAPTER 1

RUTHIE'S STORY

For the last ten years there have been so many ups and down in my life. Mostly downs. I was frightened; I was disappointed; I was lost.

First, I went through a nasty divorce. Since then, I have been trying to raise my children on my own. During this time, I was also helping to nurse my mother through her six-year battle with cancer. She died four years ago. I missed her terribly. More recently, my hair was ripped out of my scalp by a chemically damaging hair-care product that was supposed to stop frizzies and curls. Weeks, then months passed, and it wasn't growing back. Doctors had me believing I had a life-threatening disease. I lost one job because, being hairless, I frightened the people with whom I worked.

Then, I lost my next job because I was being sexually harassed by my boss. He refused to stop and I refused to put up with it. He began stalking me. He was showing up everywhere. Eventually, I even sold my van to make it more difficult for him to follow me. Communicating this horrendous situation to the police was embarrassing, difficult and demeaning. Lawyers confused me. What were my rights? Did restraining orders work? I was suffering emotionally. I was still in mourning over my mother. I was frightened, anxious and worried constantly. I was at the bottom of my world.

I went to a priest whose words gave me no consolation. He sent me to a psychologist who was helping me "sort out" my problems. I was also beginning to see Stevan Thayer, the developer of Integrated Energy Therapy.® I joined a meditation group at his Center. I was trying everything. I prayed I would eventually find someone to talk to who could help me and possibly give me hope. I prayed and prayed and prayed. I was sick with worry and paralyzed by fear.

Then, one evening, weeks later, while I was in the Zen meditation group, I began to cry my eyes out over an emotional hurt someone else in the room was feeling. I knew I was extremely sensitive to the people around me. I felt what they felt. I was crying so hard, it took awhile before I heard the whirring sound of a ceiling fan that had, for some reason, suddenly been turned on. Usually the room was very quiet and still. I could feel the air currents moving faster and faster around my head and across my face. The whirring and humming sounds were growing louder and louder.

Finally, I opened my eyes and looked up to see what was going on. Through my tears, I saw the movement of what I thought was a fan but was actually, unbelievably, most wondrously, the whirring of the wings of an angel! I could see, hovering right next to my cheek, a little, sweet chubby angel with wings like a hummingbird. He was smiling and flapping his wings very hard so I would notice him. I was so astounded I stopped crying. His presence was radiating happiness directly into me! I began to feel relief. For a few brief moments, he gave me a safe harbor. No tears. No pain. No fear. Just wonder and amazement.

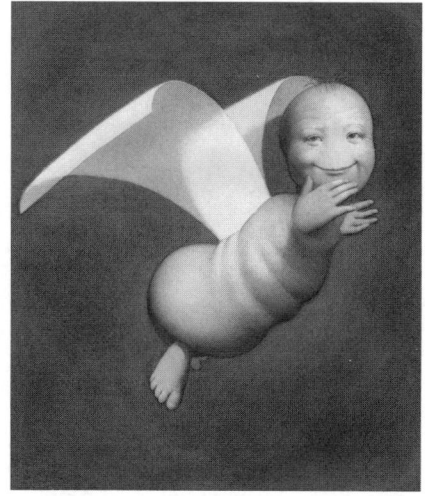

I started to question what was happening and realized, on top of all my other problems, I was probably "cracking up," completely "out to lunch," otherwise known as "going off the deep end." But I did stop hurting for a little while. I dried my eyes and left the room. Everyone had seen me crying—how embarrassing. What could I say? "Pardon me, guys, but an angel with hummingbird wings was sitting with me." Oh well, I thought, tomorrow is my individual session with Stevan. I'll try to tell him. He is so compassionate. At least he will attempt to understand.

The morning was for me, as usual, full of fear. Will I be safe today? Will my hair ever look decent? Will I ever stop remembering about the frights of cancer and my mother's long, horrible battle? Will the court system stop my ex-boss from ever harassing me again?

Later in the afternoon, I was finally in the waiting room of Stevan's office. No one else was there. I was extremely tense—waiting, worrying, obsessing. Then, suddenly, I sensed that I was not alone. Someone else, somehow, had entered the room. I panicked. How long had this person been watching me? I looked up to see who was staring so intently at me. Then, I froze like a deer in the path of a bright light. There, right in front of me, stood a creature as tall as the ceiling. It was staring right into my eyes. I felt the eyes emanating like halogen lights, sending love into me. I was awestruck. I felt touched from somewhere I had never felt before.

I could clearly see that he was masculine and naked, but without genitals. He was one being, but his presence was as strong as a thousand men. He was absolutely beautiful, like a piece of sculpture. This presence was stopping time for me. I did not know if it was night or day—and it did not matter!

The feeling and message of the presence was that he stands between me and anything that threatens me, because he is love and strength. Suddenly, I saw his wings! The wings hit the ceiling and spread out to the floor. He looked solid, but his wings were transparent. He was wonderful. His hands, so perfect, so large, revealing he has the strength to support me and everything on Earth. I wanted the moment to go on forever; then I heard Stevan call out, "I'll see you now, Ruthie."

I tried to stand up and somehow managed to walk into the therapy room. He casually asked, "How are you doing?" Still stunned, I gathered the courage to tell the truth. Certain I was putting myself on the line once more, certain I would not be accepted, I gasped, "Stevan, I saw an angel in your lobby." He replied with grace and confidence, "How wonderful. Did you get his name?"

"No, Stevan. I didn't. I was too busy staring."

"Next time ask, Ruthie."

When I left his office, I wondered, was he humoring me? I have always been a skeptic. He is just being nice. I must be dreaming all this. Or hallucinating. How can this be? I never messed with drugs in college. I never smoked pot. I don't even drink. So why am I seeing things? Oh well, I sighed, unable to make sense of all this, tomorrow I go to the shrink.

The next day, I was driving in the van on my way to the shrink. I'm worrying: Should I tell her that I'm seeing angels? She'll think I am more of a lunatic than before! Now I can add seeing angels to my repertoire. Cute. She'll probably put me on some drug for hallucinating. Or she'll send me to a bigger shrink than she. My obsessing began again. I can't tell a shrink this stuff. I need advice. I need help. I need consolation.

Then, in my rearview mirror, I noticed someone moving behind me inside the van. Terrified, I looked again. Just what I need! The angel I saw the day before was sitting in the back seat! I was in moving traffic, obsessing, with an angel in my rearview mirror looking at me. Now I was certain I had cracked up. This was it! I drove to a red light and stopped: **The angel got up, walked to the front of my big van, knelt down next to me and rested his hand on my shoulder!**

Again, I could feel his strength. I felt his protective power and his overwhelming love. Tears of joy poured from my eyes. At the next red light, I turned my van around and drove back home knowing this angel was not a dream. This angel is real and he loves me.

After this experience, my outlook on everything began to change. My old fears and anxieties began to subside, but new fears popped up! Was I really seeing angels? Did an angel actually touch me? How could this be? For a person who had never had any interest or any attraction to angels, this was very new, very extraordinary.

I was not raised on angel stories. I never bought angel ornaments for my Christmas tree. I never bought greeting cards or stationery with angels printed on them. I never read angel books. I thought angels were absurd, a fantasy, like the Wizard of Oz. Ridiculous. Yet here I am seeing and being touched by angels!

Since childhood and through my early adulthood, I had occasionally seen spirits. Usually they were brief visions of older, extended-family members and friends who had passed on. These visions would occur once and lasted only long enough for me to recognize who the spirit was or what the spirit looked like. Then I would know who to give the message to that their loved one was safe and still alive—somewhere, somehow. Often I did not know beforehand that they had died. If I did not know who they were, someone in my immediate family would recognize who the spirit was from my description of what I had seen. These visions were spontaneous and infrequent. I never thought much of this and did not try to contact spirits on my own.

In the days that followed my first angelic encounters, I realized that I had, in fact, a few weeks earlier, started seeing spirits once again. Only I did not know who or what they were. Remember, at the time, I was being followed and I was scared. Fear makes the imagination run wild. So I dismissed a lot of what I had seen.

Very soon, however, I discovered the angels were not temporary visitors. In the weeks that followed, I continued to see the first two angels and other angels were beginning to reveal themselves to me. I was continually awestruck and confused. They were not "just" visions. They were not illusions. They were real. I began to accept that I was seeing angels and that I wasn't hallucinating. Each time I saw an angel, my eyes were open and I could feel their presence. I had a growing sense that they wanted something, and I wanted to see if I could somehow communicate with them. Most of all, I wanted to understand what was going on. By now I no longer had any doubts; I knew they were truly angels.

I decided I had better write these experiences down, so I began writing and describing their appearance. I even attempted to draw them but they are so human-like yet unhuman; I could not do it. My frustration was unbearable. Then I met a woman who suggested I try automatic writing. The idea is to sit in a quiet place with a candle, pen and paper so your hands can get messages that the spirits or angels write. Yeah sure, I thought, and next I can be on *Star Trek.* The idea seemed absurd.

But at home, alone at night, the urge to communicate and the feeling of not being alone haunted me. One night, very late, I decided I would prove this writing method to be nonsense. I would do everything possible to connect with these angels and determine what was really going on here.

While other people were at the movies, watching sports on TV, and socializing, I was totally preoccupied with angels. Oh, you're crazy, Ruth, I thought. Yet I was positive I was seeing angels. Each time I saw one, they'd come back, three and four times or more, appearing just as they did the time before.

I chose a candle. I picked up a couple of matchbooks and, with some hesitation, pulled out a match. Throughout my entire life I could not light a match. This is one fact known in my family and by my close friends: Ruthie cannot light a match, Ruthie will burn her hands. Some people can't dance. Some can't grow flowers and plants. Some are color blind. I can't light matches.

I took a deep breath and struck the matchhead against the back of the book, wondering how many matches I'd have to go through. The match burst into flame on the very first try! I was incredulous; I lit the candle. Then I got ready to put a pen in my hand and to ask the angels to write for me. I felt glad my children were asleep. To see their mother doing this would have been comical to them.

My hands are small and not very powerful physically. I decided to use a marker pen with a felt tip to make it harder. I will close my eyes for this hocus-pocus. I will put the pen in my left hand because I am right-handed. I will make this difficult for the angels. This will be impossible to do and, once and for all, I can abandon this craziness, I thought.

So there I sat in the dark, candle lit, paper held down with my right hand, pen in my wrong hand, waiting for the writing to begin...if it will. I closed my eyes, and I felt overwhelming fright because I began to feel the angels in the room! After

don't drag a man along
find an equal
tell the one you
trust what the
problem
is
really
fix it

less than a minute, my left hand began to feel strange. The flat part of my hand had pressure on it. What was happening was the one thing I could never have imagined. Pressure was being placed on the back of my palm and the base of my hand, in the exact points that would force my fingers to move and write!

Very slowly the pen began writing, as pressure on my hand moved from one place to another, forming words and lines. I was very amazed but at ease, as I sensed that I was doing what I should be doing. The pen kept moving slowly up and down. I couldn't believe that this was really happening. I knew I wasn't moving the pen. After a while, I stopped in total awe. I looked down. Then, the most eye-opening event happened. Apparently, I wasn't supposed to stop. For while the pen lay in my relaxed hand, the angel picked up the pen and started pulling and pushing it while dragging my hand along! I could not believe my own eyes—or hands. I tried to stop the writing, but the pen was pulled even harder. Again and again I resisted; again and again the pen was pushed and pulled to form words. Strong angels! The message was insisting on

on how to get through this
life together one and
all in
peace
share
angels in unison

coming through like a baby who wants to be born. I couldn't stop it. (Just now, while writing this part of the story, an angel told me to tell you, "Our messages are as urgent as a baby that wants to be born. They can be delivered in many ways. Ask for them, Ruthie.")

After a while, the writing stopped on its own. I began to read what was on the page. The writing was all over the place—and messy—but there were complete words and sentences. Then I realized the message was personal, and I was able to read most of the words. This was great—they knew me; they needed me. They had messages for me. I had found a way to communicate with them. Later, I learned that if I asked them a question, they would answer. I was talking with angels!

Every night I could not wait for the phone to stop ringing and get late enough for everyone to be in bed so I could go downstairs to the kitchen, turn out the light and write with angels. Every night I had a meeting with angels. This was better than anything else I could possibly have been doing. I felt like a kid on the sly, staying up late to watch TV. I had a book of personal and healing messages. The angels' words and their presence gave me hope, security and love. My anxieties and fears began to diminish.

A few weeks later, I started to receive messages for friends and acquaintances. As new people came into my life, their angels often gave me messages for them. I also began receiving messages for people I have known casually for years. I'm always compelled to give the messages to the people they are meant for, even if it is awkward. After reading their messages and getting the advice or help they need, these individuals are so appreciative. Casual acquaintances are now deep, loving friends. Angels bring me love!

Soon after this, I had a vision. It was of a little boy, approximately four years old, holding a white book in his hands. On the book in small letters are printed the words: ANGEL TALK. My automatic writing has become clearer, stronger, easier. I learned I can write with my right hand and receive the messages telepathically. The angels also began giving me their names: Angel Ariel, Humanity, Angel With Hummingbird Wings, and others. The messages started to begin with the words, "Please tell all people" and end with, "Now tell all people."

Now, on my way to visiting my clients for Integrated Energy Therapy sessions, I telepathically receive messages from angels for these individuals. I stop and write them down. Even new clients are often greeted with an entire letter meant for them. I am surprised and so are they! "Pardon me," I say, "I know you wanted me to do energy work with you, but on the way over here, an angel dictated this letter for you." Very often, I will be with a client in his home or place of business and an angel will present itself for me to give the client information. Many people have angels just waiting to connect with them. The spirits of departed loved ones have also been appearing more often with messages to pass on to the client's family.

The writings at night are becoming longer, more poetic, more loving, more universal. The vision of the boy with the book is occurring more frequently. He is holding a book that is small enough for a child to hold, with large print so that older people can read it easily. Messages for public figures, celebrities and more and more people fill pages in my journals. The book is taking shape without my help at all. There are now sections with specific themes, moods and styles. There is even a children's section. After four months, I have nearly one hundred messages and pieces, and the book feels complete.

Every night, no matter what is going on, I have messages to write. During this time angels are presenting themselves to me more and more. I have begun to be able to hear their messages whenever and wherever they show up.

I've seen or received messages from angels who are flying behind ambulances, hanging on people walking by, in restaurants, in offices, in houses, in a laundromat, in stores, in churches, in synagogues, in parking lots, on a bench in the mall, on a Nautilus machine in a health club, on

will you please tell me why you do not notice me
I fill you up with a new day each morning
I put starlight in your eyes at evening
I turn your eyes to the Sunday warmth
I place your hands on life each day
I stand before you with open arms you are
so caught up in the everyday ritual that
*   you fail*
to see me seeing you
archangel ariel

a camping trip, at a dinner party, in cars, in a field, on the side of the road, at the beach, in the forest. Sometimes they are around specific people; other times they just watch.

I've written messages on envelopes, bank deposit slips, menus, business cards, newspapers, paper towels from the ladies' room, and on pizza parlor placemats: one for eating, one for writing—anything I can get my hands on when the messages start to come.

Today, I can tell you when the Tiny Angel With Hummingbird Wings visits me, he is announcing the impending arrival of a higher angel. They, and all the other angels, give me words they wish to spread among many people. They are so very happy to communicate with all of us.

Through writing, visions and visits, I have been given all kinds of information and messages to "share with other people on Earth." Angels write with me. Everywhere. Anytime. Spontaneously. Why? For what reason? Because they love us! They love you.

CHAPTER 2

ANGEL VISIONS

Over the course of a most unusual and wondrous year, I have seen and heard many different angels and I continue to meet new ones. Each has a distinctive presence—unique physical characteristics combined with a feeling that mirrors their physical appearance. If the angelic message is for peace and calm, the feeling and appearance of the angel will be peaceful and calm. If the message is meant to convey strength, the angelic appearance will depict and emanate strength. The visions I see and the presence I feel instantly indicate to me the nature of my soon-to-arrive message. Some angels appear solo; some arrive in small groups; others quite literally stand out in a crowd.

The three best adjectives to describe angels would be, and these words were given to me by the angels themselves:

perfect,

defined,

delicate.

I am giving you the descriptions of the angels I have seen. I believe we cannot see their true form fully. What we see is the angel's personal translation, from the spiritual realm to the physical realm, enabling us to comprehend them.

Their most distinguishing physical characteristic is their wings. (This is the reason, when the encounters began to take place, that I knew I was seeing angelic spirits rather than human spirits.) Typically, the wings are transparent, very lightweight and come in different shapes and sizes. Some are turned upward, some downward, and they vary greatly in detail. The wings are not bird-like as seen in many wall hangings and Christmas decorations. I don't think they're used for flying, but for hovering.

Their bodies or forms always appear to be human-like in some aspects. For instance, they all have faces but they do not necessarily have fully human-looking torsos or limbs. I believe they reflect human characteristics and forms to mirror us, so we can relate to them. Sometimes these characteristics are very clearly seen, almost highlighted. Other times they are just slightly suggested or hidden by what they are wearing, by their wings, or by the light they emanate. I have come to understand that these details vary in clarity to emphasize the message they are trying to convey. Often their eyes are a prominent feature—large and seemingly able to radiate thoughts and energy.

The other physical features that are often clearly seen are their feet and hands. They are simply exquisite and much, much larger than human feet and hands. I believe these features are emphasized to convey an essential aspect of who the angels are and the work they do. In their poetry and messages they say their work involves helping us to "build a tower to God," to strengthen the connection between the physical and spiritual planes. They also refer to us as their "Earth flowers." Their role is to help cultivate all life on Earth—humans, animals and plants.

Angels have no gender as we know it. I have come to understand that they will look and sound either masculine or feminine in accordance with the energy and content of the message they are sending.

There are two other physical features common to most angels. They usually have hair— although it is not hair as we know it. Their hair is extremely fine, like rare silk threads. It is lighter than air and flows and floats around them.

Angels also have skin—but, again, it is not skin as we know it. The texture of their skin is so refined that it appears to be a different substance altogether.

Each angel has a unique voice. It is through their voices that they have delivered every message in this book. Usually I will see them with my human eyes, or with my inner vision, in which case a scene will fill my mind and persist until I notice the angel who is trying to get my attention. There are times when a sighting or vision does not accompany the words I begin to hear. Because their voices are so distinctive, if I am already familiar with the angel, I am able to identify who is speaking even though I may not be seeing them at the time.

When I am about to see or hear an angel, I detect a presence in the room and the atmosphere around me becomes extremely calm. Then, I sense someone or something approaching because the feeling grows stronger. Then, the feeling becomes an incredibly detailed, living vision. The illustrations in this section really capture what I see. If other people are with me, their speech seems to slur so I can no longer hear what they are saying. Other times, the people around me are distracted by something long enough for me to hear what the angel is trying to say. Sometimes the message is repeated over and over until it catches my attention. Often I am compelled to write it down immediately, using any paper I can find. Many times the lines won't leave me alone until I begin to write down what I am hearing. Then, as I write, the message flows.

My publisher wants to know why I don't run out of the room screaming. How come I'm not terrified by a hairless, emaciated

life form hanging onto a person in the street or s[...]
living room? There's nothing to be frightened o[...]
wonderful things from each of them, and eac[...]
thing different.

So, here is what I see—my visions of the[...]
given me messages for you, for all of us, w[...]
repeatedly that they are available and waiting[...]
them.

Angel Ariel

Think of Angel Ariel when you need a protector. Through his presence, he gives a solid surge of monumental mental and physical support. His primary message is: "I am strong for you." While some angels bring the message and energy of love and gentleness, Ariel does this and more.

Ariel is almost nine feet tall. His wings are gigantic, rounded and transparent. They rise upward behind him and extend downward below his heels. These wings are not feathered or bird-like in any way. His stance and presence are of extreme poise, grace, beauty and strength. His gaze is acute, strong and compassionate.

He wears nothing, has no genitals, yet appears very masculine in form when he reveals his presence to me. His voice also sounds masculine. Ariel consistently displays an awesome masculine strength in order, I believe, for me to "get the point and get the picture" of the power and strength that is available from the angelic realm.

I am always awestruck when I see Ariel; he is a masterpiece,

a work of art, perfectly combining both beauty and strength. Every muscle and bone of his body is sculpted and well-defined, like a person whose muscles were toned from swimming. He has a long neck, broad shoulders and a slim waist. His arms and legs are very long. His hands and feet are unusually large.

Ariel has long, dark brown hair, parted off center, that curls and flows well past his shoulders. His hair is fine and airy. His face is angular and well-sculpted. The eyebrows are bushy yet finely lined. He has large, dark, almond-shaped eyes with huge pupils. His nose is chiseled like a model's. Ariel's lips are big and full, well-proportioned to his face, yet substantial and turned up at the ends. His mouth is closed. His chin is square and completes the perfectly designed face. Ariel's skin cannot be likened to human skin: the refined texture is beyond description. His touch conveys amazing yet gentle strength.

Overall he has the graceful appearance of a ballerina and the posture of a warrior. He has an extremely strong expression. It is not an exaggeration when I say that within his singular presence he appears to possess the power of a thousand human men. Such is the magnitude of the strength he projects. Ariel's mere presence would stop an army. Remember him when you need a protector.

Tiny Angel With Hummingbird Wings

The Tiny Angel With Hummingbird Wings is the angel with the million-dollar smile. He comes very close to me, bringing the message and energy of happiness. He says: "Notice me." "Look up." "Dry your eyes." "Smile." "Do not be afraid." Often he puts me on alert: "Pay attention." "Look." "Listen." "Come this way, for other angels are about to talk." He is a contact messenger for other angels. When I see him, I have come to know that within the next three days, a bigger, more powerful angel will bring me a message. The Tiny Angel With Hummingbird Wings brings the message that I will be loved by this angel and have a more powerful connection. "Be ready, Ruthie," he says. He flaps his wings near the left side of my face. It is impossible not to notice him.

This is one of the first angels I encountered, and it is the most unusual looking. He floats horizontally. You can barely see his wings because they move so rapidly (like a hummingbird's wings). The body is asexual, small (less than two feet in size) and rotund like a little blimp. The body looks squashed and wrinkled because of the many overlapping folds of fatty skin. It has no arms or legs but does have hands and feet.

The large smile he wears fills and shapes his entire face. Laugh lines deeply mark his cheeks and forehead. Because of his crinkled-up smile, his eyes appear to be half-closed. He has big friendly eyes, with no eyebrows or eyelashes. There are small wisps of hair near his brow. Otherwise, his head is large, round and bald.

You might be tempted, because of his size and shape, to liken him to a cherub or Cupid type of angel—those baby angels depicted throughout history. I cannot make this analogy, however, because he is so unusual looking. This angel also shares in the work of bringing people together to meet and to receive the messages and the help they need.

Angel Lady in the Silver Cage Dress

An angel of indescribable beauty, Angel Lady in the Silver Cage Dress, appears whenever I am in fear or distress. She flashes and blinks her light above me until she gets my attention. She sends the message, "Calm down, Ruthie. Everything will be okay." I am amazed when she is with me; she is magnificent to look at; and her presence has a totally calming effect. This Angel Lady in the Silver Cage Dress radiates the energy of well-being and confidence. She envelops you with the air and feeling of absolute safety. Her primary message is: "Have no fear, you are safe." Her role, through her presence and words, is to remind us that there is more going on around us than we perceive—she is a sentry of calm amidst chaos.

This angel has a very feminine face and is petite—only four feet in length. She is extremely ethereal and transparent. She shows herself through beams of light that are very bright, silvery and yellow, almost gold. These rays of light are all around her, and she flashes like a neon light that is brighter than the day's sun. She has short, yellow, square-cut hair, with halos rising above her that look like fluorescent tubes of yellow light. She appears very still and quiet, like an inanimate object, yet she emanates a profound sense of peace.

This angel hovers above the ground, standing erect, and looks down with eyelids half-closed. Her eyes are peaceful. Her mouth is pursed with perfect bow-shaped lips. You can see the tips of her feet under her dress. Her hands are often clasped in front of her triangular-shaped dress, which is transparent like a

silver spider web with the sun shining through it. Of all the angels, her appearance is the closest to the traditional rendition of angels on Christmas ornaments.

Piggyback Angel

This angel always appears in masculine form. He is tall, thin, wispy and waif-like. The Piggyback Angel rides on a distressed, isolated person's back. He hugs and holds. His long legs either wrap around a person's torso or dangle in the air. His head rests on the person's head, his arms hug the neck and shoulders. He is weightless and has no muscles. He has big upward-pointing wings that are covered with fine angel skin.

The Piggyback Angel is a very serious angel. His presence is intense and compassionate. There are many Piggyback Angels. They are here to console people who are lost in some way. This angel is acutely concerned for the person he is with. His face and demeanor appear sorrowful because he is so empathetic to the person's distress and because he wishes the person to know of his presence. This angel has an air of great patience and often looks as if he has been waiting a lifetime for the person to notice him. He communicates his messages telepathically.

I have seen the Piggyback Angel many times. Here are some instances: on a businessman's shoulders riding in a relaxed position like a jockey; hugging a mother with three kids; and clinging to a serviceman's back. More than once, on a crowded street, I have seen these angels coming and going riding on people's shoulders.

Angel Flying in the Forest

Angel Flying in the Forest is a guide and guardian, huge, loving and peaceful, who flies silently and hovers effortlessly. As I walked through the trees, this angel was flying behind me. How long was he there before I noticed him? As I write this, his presence approaches me as I think about him. He has told me to tell you that he leads when a person cannot find his way; he follows when a person is searching. His message is that he will always help us find our way. He wears a long, flowing, white shroud-like garment and his hands and feet are proportionately many times larger than a human's. He is one of many Angels Flying in the Forest.

Angels in the Woods

I have encountered a variety of angels who can be found in the woods and forest. Their role is to guard our natural habitats and connect with us. They are delightful and their presence extends the energy of well-being throughout the air and towards all they see and guard.

Angels in the Woods appear to have their own little culture or colony. These angels seem only to know love and are not concerned with the outside world. They are busy with their work of guarding and tending the woodlands. The Angels in the Woods sit in trees like little kids or monkeys. While they laugh and play, their long legs dangle in the air and their upward-pointed wings flutter. The bodies of these angels are bony and skinny. They have big heads and faces.

Although I have only seen them in heavily wooded areas, they have communicated to me when I have been elsewhere. This was very surprising at first. Suddenly the air around me becomes saturated with the scent of pines. After a few minutes, a picture of the Angels in the Woods and what they are doing will flash across my mind. Then they begin to talk.

For some reason that I have yet to understand, when I see this colony of angels, they are often accompanied by another spiritual being. This being is not an angel, it does not have wings and does not move. It looks somewhat like an Old World holy statue. I do know that this being is **not** the soul of a departed loved one trying to convey a message to my friends or clients. Perhaps it is a saint or a master. Perhaps it is a teacher or some advanced soul who has graduated to work within the angelic realm.

Three Lady Angels That Float and Sing

The Three Lady Angels That Float and Sing are like the pure white light of a prism. With blond hair so light yellow and barely visible, they look like albino triplets. Their mouths are big, round and open, while the eyes are very dark, almost black, with no whites in the eyes. They have no eyebrows and I see no arms, hands or feet. The three heads cling to each other like love birds; they share a huge yellow halo; and they have big smiles. Always together, their white, billowy gowns float like tents and fall in folds. Their job is to guard and protect and they send messages of love. They float and sing because they are so happy to bring love and peace to all of us. I have seen this triad in ceilings, over groups of people in a field, over an ambulance and at a crowded bus stop.

Humanity

Humanity is an angel devoted to the arts. He touches people who are on the verge of a creative energy burst or in the midst of a creative endeavor meant to serve the world. He is attracted to eloquent speaking. I have sensed Humanity standing with parishioners in church. I also communicated with Humanity for an individual who is now recognizing that he is a gifted painter. This angel is also with a woman who is preparing to educate many about sculpting. Humanity gave me pieces for this book and continues to give me messages concerning creativity. There are almost enough of Humanity's messages now to compile another book. He says he is not ready to be described yet. "But please," he says, "heed my words." He speaks throughout the universe.

Angels That Mind Our Precious Souls

The Angels That Mind Our Precious Souls are a heavenly, peaceful gathering of angels with outstretched arms and huge, perfectly-shaped hands. The first three to nine angels are clearly visible standing in front of long columns of other angels, each with a distinct look and each dressed slightly differently. Each angel has long hair and wings so large they overlap each other. Their halos add a glow to their huge, expressive eyes. Each winged being carries his own message and intentions for Earth. They fly and hover with such power and strength that they confer a feeling of total security. They speak in prose and poetry, and despite the large group, they convey a feeling of quiet, calm, stillness and peace.

Cameo Appearances

Occasionally, a new angel would appear to me with a beautiful name and his own message and quickly depart. Sometimes, a lovely, sweet voice would whisper words to me and identify itself as an angel. Throughout this book, there are many different mentions and credits to angels that made a contribution only once. And still more came!

Angel Glowing Yellow is bright, intense and glowing, like the yellow part of a pilot light on a gas stove. **Angel With Outstretched Arms, Spirit Angel, Little Angel, Your Loving Angel, A Loving Angel, Angel At the End of a Long Tunnel, Angel With a Smile That Knows** and **Dancing Angels** each

made a cameo appearance. Other angels, each with different voices and similar names, spoke to me and identified themselves as: **Many Angels, Many Angels in Unison, Angels Speak in Unison, Hungry Angels** and more, who identified themselves solely as **Angels.** Each day I invite the possibility that soon they will return and "talk" us all another book!

Enjoy *Angel Talk.*

CHAPTER 3

LESSONS ON POETIC EXISTENCE

Fear

Fear is the overriding attitude that there is an end; that

there is a limit to your innermost desires and dreams. Know

the absence of fear is a clear pathway to the universe and

all it offers which is boundless, endless.

Angel Ariel

Free Will

Free will is that which leads us along the path directly

to soul. Soul thrives on free will and always returns to its

natural state; that of alliance with spirit.

Angel Ariel

Soul Shine

When your love creates a smile,

When your attention sparks a fire,

When your touch manifests heightened awareness,

When your eyes emote waves into imagination,

When your presence fills another with happiness,

You have created soul-shine.

 *An Angel Glowing Yellow*

The prayers we send to God are gathered by the Angels

and delivered to a place far beyond our imagination. Each

prayer is recognized, acknowledged and answered in its

due time, in God's way.

Angel Ariel

The precious drops of blood that pulse within our bodies are akin to the spiritual waters of the universe. We are all one; the oceans, rivers, blood within our veins. We all have a path to follow and the moon's gentle pull, the sun's nourishing warmth know every drop of life as equal. The torrential intent of the river's path, the high and low tides of ocean's current, the heartbeats of blood through our bodies; all eternally flow in the eyes of God.

Sleep peacefully,

Angel Ariel

Everyone is a star in the universe

 *Many Angels in Unison*

On Stars

In the heavens out so far,

You can barely see,

Shines a star looking down,

To the place that you call me,

You watch that star so sparkling,

Like the light inside your heart,

That star in the heavens beaming,

Has been you from your very start!

There are Angels watching us from every corner of
the universe!

 Three Lady Angels that Float and Sing

Star Talk

The next time a star shines through your window, and catches your attention, notice the blazing intent of its shine. Rays of illuminating light sparkling with only one objective; for total attention of the love object: you. Know it is an accompaniment to the all-knowing, God blessed love forever flaming within you. Just as the star shines upon you, you in turn, shine upon the star.

Remember this the next time a star shines through your window.

A star that shines within your soul is as bright as the stars of the universe. You are one of them!

An Angel Rides Piggyback on your Shoulders

A Message to Ordinary People:

No matter what your outer appearance may seem to be,

You are a shining star in the eyes of God.

There be no ordinary people.

God loves you as His Children.

Angels deliver this message.

Angel Ariel

Kings and Queens Wear Velvet

Line your prayers with velvet,

And place your heart with Angels,

For safekeeping.

In God's eyes, within every soul, on Earth,

There lives a King and Queen.

*Angel Lady in the
Silver Cage Dress*

The universe picks up its messages.

 *Spirit Angel*

CHAPTER 4

YOUR PERSONAL JOURNEY

n Angel asks:

"Can we really know what we want and where we are going on this journey?"

An Angel answers:

"All we can know is to follow our path. Have no fear. Be assured what we need and where we travel is provided for along our life's way.

If we make an effort, the smallest effort, to open up to the beginning experience, the invitation will present itself and the gala of life will begin!"

An Angel asks:

"Where you go? How you go? When you go?"

An Angel answers:

"Unimportant to know. Just know it will happen. Is there a sky above you? Is there rich soil below you? Are there bodies of water to quench your thirst? Are there trees to walk among? Does the breeze brush against your skin? Does your heart beat with the universe?"

All the Angels respond:

Of course!

 *Many Angels*

When a human is on his personal journey, know he walks forward. This is the only way Angelic spirit will lead and guide him. The divine truth is waiting to be unfolded, in his presence, as he continues down his path. The idea of turning back meandering to the right or left, (if you will), is unheard of because divine spirit guides the path.

As he is gently pulled in one direction, inspiration and truth will replace areas in life that once held the obscure, that once held fear. The acceptance of Angelic presence in existence comes with finally knowing and feeling the gentle pull of a loving spirit beckoning you to step to the path of the true reason for living.

To feel lightness of wings likened to a baby's breath. To feel brightness of inspiration within the power behind one million stars in the galaxy shining on your soul in unison. To feel a love overcome your very being like a blanket on a wintry night enfolding you in the warmth of an embrace unimaginable in your personal realm, up to this point in your life.

And then you know. And then you feel. And then you live with a love that supports and nurtures you to exalted heights basking in the floating, soaring, enlightening realization of the higher exalted love of an Angel in your very existence.

Know your Angel.
Love your Angel.
Live your Angel.

We are with you through all eternity.

Angel Ariel

Perception is Deception

Break away from despair!

Your mind does not perceive universally.

It perceives its own reflection which is deception. Break

away from despair. Know it does not intend to hurt. It

intends only to direct you to the lowest point of emotions

so you may turn and soar only higher.

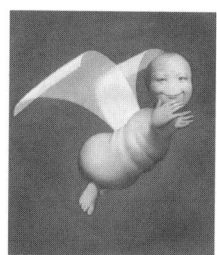

Tiny Angel with
Hummingbird Wings

Perception is Deception

Break away from the idea that all you perceive is but all you may attain in this life. Perception is a narrow view of one small corner in a vast universe with more turns and alternatives just waiting for you. As you attempt to grasp for more, you will be rewarded in ways so personal to your individual soul. Perception is a great deception.

It only goes as far as your own two eyes.

It only goes as far as the corner of your mind.

It only goes as far as your own mind-view.

Perception is a storybook,

Awareness is the truth.

Perception is fiction,

Awareness is non-fiction.

Perception is the last stop on the railroad,

Awareness is getting off the train and flying,

With wings, the rest of your way.

Perception is a room with four corners.

Awareness is a room with no corners.

Perception is the deception that all you perceive is all there is. Keep in mind the idea: if you are open and aware, perception fades away and awareness is endless.

 *Angels Flying Through the Forest*

Perception is Deception

Safe. Still. Timeless.

No beginning and no end.
A dimension where the movie does not end.

This life seems long and tedious. In some instances, you
perceive your journey has taken you farther down your path
only to find a new mountain to overcome. Do not perceive.
This is a fool's mind. Only know your efforts are not in vain.
All trails, no matter how fruitless, no matter how dead, no
matter how zero to naught they may seem, all lead your
soul forward.

Perhaps once ago the path was crossed,
By you and by many more,
The path has changed and so have you,
Your next life will open the door.

 Truth from the Comic Angel

$\mathcal{T}$ake this time to know when the Angels come to you, all time stands still. All doors will open and all places on Earth are nowhere but in your mind. Your spirit is carried to another plane, another dimension where time and space are stationary in God's realm and in God's eyes.

Is this life but a second, a passing thought, a nod of head in any direction for one slight moment? Is this life eons of earth-rotation with no final destination? This life is akin to all other lives. We share these lives and live them over and over again.

The person you meet on a crowded street and casually walk by;
Possible you have met before in another life.
Wonder why?

Angels intervene. Angels step in. Angels involve themselves when all your options are spent, when all your guesses brought no answer, when all your roads lead to the same place and the place is not where you long to be. Relax in guiding hands. Walk down path Angels lead you. Go forward with Angels following each step of your way.

Feel embryonic bliss enclosed in Angel wings. Turn your face towards God and feel brushes of love upon your face. Pour tears of elation when your eyes unite with the glance of an Angel.

 *Angel with Outstretched Arms*

We want to tell you about growing and time

Size and physical strength are the only methods we have to display to humans that their path is going forward. Physical perception is a non-reality. Your minds have the ability to evolve at a speedier rate than your physical self. How long does it take a tree to grow large? How long does it take a river to change its path? How long does it take a glacier to travel? Much, in Earth turns.

You all have the ability to transport your minds, your thoughts and your very personal ideas further than you have the ability to understand this solid concept:

The imagination is the reality.

 This little lesson comes from the love of a little Angel.

We want to tell you about growing and time

Take a walk through a garden and notice the way flowers live life. They open petals. They spread pollen. They produce new flowers from their roots. Although flowers bloom very quickly, in Earth turns, a short span of life, they bloom proudly and with all their power upwards towards sun. All petals open to receive God-warmth. Flowers live in the now. Notice their entire span of blooming life is perfectly natural and beautiful and graceful from beginning to end.

Take a lesson from a flower and an Angel.

Just live and bloom to your fullest.

On Defining Time

Please tell all the people our attention only focuses on them. Have faith in this fact: Angels fly around, above, beneath a soul as it carries out the path designed in Earth realm. If you feel overlooked, tossed to the side, passed by, move to the side. Let that feeling escape. Know there is more. All is well for you. You are safe in redeeming your Self for more.

We hold your hands. We support your spirit. We are present when there is no way to turn. When the Earth options appear bankrupt, as you feel the final door of opportunity close in your Earth face, when even stepping backward or retiring is no longer a valid exit, be assured there are more paths, more views, to rest your hungry eyes and ever thirsty imagination upon.

Tell Earth people to look for the signs that indicate we are with them. Although the clock ticks as you walk through your Earth life, know that time only owns its significance on your planet. Time is a part of your Earth act.

Now, you will know that time has no importance, no influence in fulfilling your life path. Since your spirit has the power to be born anew each day, each sunrise, time is no longer a threat to your Earth journey. The clock ticks, but only to hear itself make noise. Listen to the quiet, and know.

Forever is for every one
Forever is
For Everyone

A ticking clock is silent
When time loses its definition.

All this from your Angel,

Angel Ariel

Notice Angels

Angels huddle in bouquets,

At the edge of a field, where the forest begins,

Angels encoiled among branches of oaks,

Chanting on the breeze,

Angels hover above an earth-being,

As he looks up for answers.

Angels That Mind
Our Precious Souls

Grasping at Angels

It is impossible to grasp for an Angel. Your hands are constantly held by Angels. Grasp is a state of mind; very fleeting, mind you. The merest thought summons an Angel to you immediately. There is more for all of you.

 *Humanity*

Angel Hands

Angel hands are ever-open to surround and support. Angel hands touch with love and divine guidance. Artistic and delicate in renditions throughout history, yet created with the strength of God; open enough to cradle the universe. Earth has yet to fully understand the immense protection contained in Angel hands. Hands of Angels enclose us peacefully as we experience longing with our earth eyes.

 *Humanity*

Earth Eyes

Earth eyes watching...waiting,

The focus is on you.

And, all ways, shall be.

Build your tower to God.

Share happiness with Angels!

(Angels sing!)

 *Humanity*

Focus

Impressions on the horizon,
As your oceans brush against the clouds.
Waves lapping, kissing,
The thirsty ages-old earth shores.

The products of a summer's growth,
These leaves top heaven-bound trees in a lover's frenzy.
A fire thrives,
With the comforting knowledge it will blaze forever.

Attempt to live your life past that horizon, at that place
where scattering waves give birth to a new shoreline each
second. Cling to each other as the leaves on that tree; all
huddled, growing towards God. All together.

We will keep safe your flame to the heavens.
Build your tower to God.
We all cry with joy!

 *Your Loving Angels*

Focus

It expends quite an effort to fathom God.

Cast to the side your earthly prizes,

And allow this vision to become clearer.

Focus.

*Angels That Mind
Our Precious Souls*

Invite Us

Angels await the human spirit to open enough for all to see. We wait for all Earth to embrace the realization there is more love, hope and joy. An ocean can redirect tide. The sun can shine all day and night. Operas may be sung on bird songs. Stars can appear affixed in circles of light like fireworks on your Fourth of July. Love can encompass a being like an electric blanket of five hundred degrees. The warmth is so enlightening that eyes will pour tears of joy, mouths will quiver with anticipation, ears will listen to the songs of God.

All a being must do is invite an Angel.

Angel Ariel

An Angel Pleads:

Please notice us!

We stand at attention in the background of your life waiting for that possible second. We await the invitation to enter your life. We may wait through your lifetimes for a soul to open his door that small inch to change his eternity. The familiar scene you play out each day of your life, perhaps hesitate and take a longer look. We are there all ready! We await our chance to step in.

There is no time in our realm. Time is still (if you will). We observe with patient love as you live on Earth days through your time. You may look a different way. You may turn a different way. You may observe a different way and finally notice us.

It only takes a second to alter an eternity.

*I*t only takes a second to alter an eternity.

Angels' Poetry

We laugh, we play	Through your Earth day,
We sing, we soar	At your Earth door,
We float, we fly	In your mind's eye,
We love, we hold	When we are told!

Invite us!

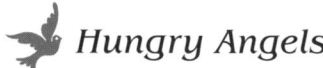 *Hungry Angels*

We Sit on the Sidelines

We sit on the sidelines and wait in the background to be called forth. Please present a situation so we may come into your life. Seek our guidance. We have so much to offer. We have so much to relate, so much to enfold into lives. Know there are more dimensions to your soul and to the life on Earth. There is a total dimension of love where a soul may exist in timeless adoring splendor. There is a dimension that emits creative forces so intense, they will soar across galaxies to the target.

Great artists, poets, composers mature in this realm before honoring Earth with the masterpieces. Da Vinci lived in this dimension for eons. There is selected space in the universe for all teachers, leaders and guides for mankind. Many attune lifetimes to claim their place in Earth history. Doctors, healers, scientists, spiritual saints have yet one more realm that fills each of these souls with the capabilities to nurture. Madame Curie and Jonas Salk are souls molded here for ages. These specific realms were created to mold these souls along their spiritual path. These realms revolve eternally in the universe readying to enlighten mankind.

A little further down the path to God, a little closer each

time, in all ways all Earth life is tended to by Him. We

Angels follow God's plans for each of you. Angels bridge

the love God sends for life on Earth. Angels carry the love

Earth sends for God straight to the source.

 *Angels Speak in Unison*

CHAPTER 5

LOVE POETRY

& UNIVERSAL MESSAGES
for ALL BEINGS

The Angel in my heart knows my love is warm,

The Angel in my heart moves the beats upon my breast,

The Angel in my heart knows I am all ways loved,

The Angel in my heart lives there.

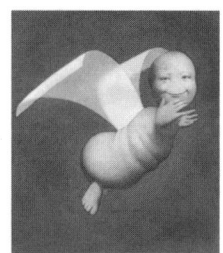

*Tiny Angel with
Hummingbird Wings*

$\mathscr{H}$is wings enter me with joy.

The stillness is one thousand deep lakes on a windless day.

The peace is one thousand babies asleep in their beds.

The joy is every bell in the universe ringing in unison.

The love is an Angel in your heart.

 *Angel Glowing Yellow*

$\mathcal{T}$he belief there is a place more serene,

Than a field of new-fallen snow,

The sensation of spring rain,

Bouncing down your body,

Yet replenishing Earth from a faraway place,

Barely hearing the satisfied sigh,

Of an infant falling into sleep,

Resting your fingers on the gaping petals of a
    flower,

In its height of bloom,

The lingering taste of a lover's kiss,

On your satisfied lips

Enfolded in the wings of an Angel.

 *Three Lady Angels that Float and Sing*

The tears pour down my cheeks in silence,

My two lips throb with fulfilled happiness,

My hands quiver with star-like energy,

My heart dances in the universe

An Angel's kiss.

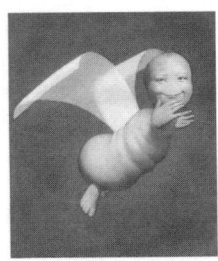

*Tiny Angel with
Hummingbird Wings*

The presence of an Angel in your life.

How calm?

How serene?

As loud as the sound snow does not make,

When it falls to Earth.

We are with you.

Angel Ariel

*I*f there was a candle in my mind,

What then, would I see?

A path to follow, search and find,

The flame that is truly me.

 Angel at the End of a Long Tunnel

Follow me to the ocean,

Follow me to the woods,

Follow me to the ethers,

Follow me to the edge of the universe.

 *Angels*

The earth is surrounded by Angels,

And some of them know you,

The earth is loved by Angels,

And all of them love you.

 *An Angel said so.*

*I*n the nest, there are some eggs,

On the tree, there are some buds,

In the lake, the fish are warm,

In the beds, the flowers bloom.

Spring comes again, just like your Angel,

After a cold long winter in your soul,

And comes again.

Angel Ariel

The ache I feel for the kiss I missed,

The pain I own for the absent caress,

The tears I spill from my empty heart,

The hope I keep for another time,

A candle burns through many turns.

Angel Lady in the
Silver Cage Dress

A crystal is my mirror,

The mirror is my soul,

A crystal is my storybook,

All my lives past unfold.

I see us in the starlight,

I dream us in my sleep,

Crystal on my own two lips,

That brush against your cheek.

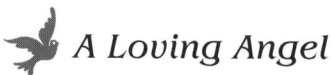 *A Loving Angel*

The master of my fate lived a time before,

The artist of my life drew my image long ago,

A vague remembrance of a vital love that past,

He returns to hold me once again.

Angel Flying in the Forest

$\mathcal{S}$culptures of your memories,

Flashbacks of your past,

It is indeed the exact sun,

That rose the time before

You are here once more.

Angel Lady in the
Silver Cage Dress

Pine cones dressing the forest floor,

Crickets filling the air with muse,

Moss encircling each base of tree,

Remember when I was you and you were me?

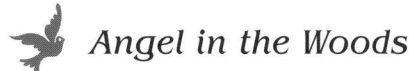 *Angel in the Woods*

The trees were big, the trees were small,

First we were little then we grew tall,

I ask you a question, you give no reply,

Full of life, then you die?

We come back again, we meet, how?

I still have a question,

So answer me now.

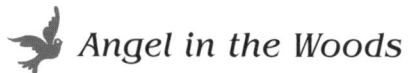 *Angel in the Woods*

Do not search for us,

We will find you.

Do not wait for us,

We are there all ready.

Do not whisper your name,

We know it well.

We have loved you forever,

Time will tell.

 *Angels*

CHAPTER 6

ANGELS ILLUMINATE LOVE

Love

Know there is a spirit realm in the universe that does nothing but love you and your fellow creatures. You are looked after and nurtured like all other life-forms on your planet. Are birds singing? Are trees reaching to heavens? Are animals content in their lairs?

Look into each one of yourselves and discover love.

Angel Ariel

The Subject is Love

There is much to be said on this subject of love. Love owns so many forms and shapes that we do not notice when love arrives. First, real love has no physical requirements. Every thing on Earth realm, no matter how it appears, owns the inherent properties to attract love. The essence of the existence, the fact that it has come into being, gives the natural ability to be loved. Do not despair, humans! Take some advice by looking into nature. Go back to your natural state creatures into being through God, just like all other creatures on your planet. Love is available to all. Put out the invitation for love to come. Do not label! Do not expect! Do not preconceive! Love will find you. Will you recognize it?

Angel Lady in the Silver Cage Dress

True Love

Love cannot fully arrive in man-form.

But two men may experience it together.

Love cannot ever fill you entirely,

But it can spill over into two beings at the same time.

Love cannot be found for you to own,

But it can be held eternities in your heart with another
being.

Remember:

Every drop of wave cresting and breaking in the surf is the
laugh of an Angel.

*Angels That Mind
Our Precious Souls*

Dear Angel Ariel,

Can we ever own love?

With respect and love,
Ruthie

An Angel Answers:

Love has no beginning and no end.

Every being we meet and love, we have loved in another life. The relationship travels to where it terminated at another time.

The heartbreak occurs when we do not allow our true emotions to live and run their course. Can we ever own love, Ruthie?

The answer to your question lives in the words: Earth Games. Stop the Earth Games and be aware of the answer.

The spirit will all ways run free.

All Earth creatures with needs and desires shall be
allowed to run free.

The weed is a flower also.
The lemon is a fruit also.
A cactus is a beautiful king in the desert sea.

Do not attempt to steal another being's freedom.
Do not judge.
This is the secret of love.
This is the secret of peace.

The spirit will all ways run free.

Angel Ariel

True Love

Let us tell you what true love is likened to
in Earth terms:

Multiple rainbows spanning the horizon of the ocean.
Waves cresting in unison with the pulse of the universe.
Sunshine in every pore of a person's being.
An awning over the emotional downpour of life,
An Angel's wing like a shed over your soul.

A ride under an Angel's wing is the sensation of flying into
the gaping mouth of the river called enlightenment that
explodes in torrents the mind-picture of a million vast sun-
sets in the pastoral valley of hope that has no beginning
and has no end; so ongoing that you must close your eyes
to the brightest light of heaven spilling love.

Angel Ariel

Why does Cupid shoot an Arrow?

The fierce, yet peaceful, power of love is keener than Cupid's arrow. Directed to the target, Cupid's arrow owns the same strength of attention and intention that Earth's gravity demonstrates constantly with God-given force. Cupid's arrow sends the love of God to you, the Earth flowers.

Remember this the next time you walk
    in a field of wild daisies.

Remember this the next time you see
    a wild daisy in your dreams.

Somewhere in the universe there is an Angel
    blooming wild daisies to celebrate His love for you.

 *Three Lady Angels that Float and Sing*

Heartache

Take this advice from Angelic messages and pass it on to Earth beings. Today, allow heartache to be the subject. Heartache is disguised as misguided love. A love aimed for a purpose but totally missing the target.

Love is lost when you conjure up the target in your mind. Love has no direction. It merely flows. It does not judge. It loves unconditionally as any mother being towards her children. Love is a natural, Love is likened to a bud appearing on a tree, after a cold, bitter, long winter. As the rays of sun, shine on it, warm it up, the bud bursts into a beautiful flower.

As you warm a heart with soul-shine, love blooms like a flower. Love occurs naturally from the warmth of the sun as the warmth in your heart. The object of your love flourishes in the warmth of your soul-shine. The object of your love basks in your soul-shine.

Heartache occurs when we misdirect our emotions toward someone or something hunting for power and we mistake it for a love-interest in our soul. This heartache is a natural part of a soul-life on Earth. It is an exercise of learning. Do not send out love to a dead tree with no buds. Only send out love where your soul may flourish.

Piggyback Angel

Heartache

Much truth dwells in heartache.

Hush and allow the noises of night creatures,

To sing you love songs.

Gild your tarnished heart.

Summon an Angel.

Piggyback Angel

The Message is Love

An Angel is my sun,

And warms me within wings of eternal love,

An Angel is my soul,

The message is steady, still,

Like a bottomless lake,

It is a bright spring day in my heart.

Accept and rejoice.

Angel Lady in the Silver Cage Dress

CHAPTER 7

ANGEL TOWERS

The Angels Build A Tower To God.

Angel Ariel

The Angels Build a Tower to God...

The Angels build a tower to God and all along that tower, stretching to the heavens, are our Earth-frail hands passionately clutching and grasping for the word of enlightenment.

Meanwhile, our souls so strong, yet full in forgotten spiritual knowledge, climb courageously and effortlessly.

This is the innate knowledge that Angels of God so pastorally and naturally, hold us high. Fear not. There be no fear.

 *Words of an Angel on a Sunlit Winter's day*

The Angels Build a Tower to God...

The Angels build a tower to God. Each Angel has his destination on Earth plane. The power is so forceful that it can span an ocean, leap over a star, encircle every branch on a tree. When an Angel comes to you, be assured your unique place on Earth will be carried out, with Divine Spirit. The laugh of an Angel is as soft and gentle as a lone rain-drop on a flower petal. The will of an Angel may fill you with millions of sparks of energy. Lift your spirit and fly away, into a realm of multiple awareness, and, in all ways, love.

Angel Ariel

The Angels Build a Tower to God...

And all along that tower is a scaffold of love and strength offering an endless amount of knowledge, and definition to life. As a soul climbs higher to collect his answers, he will notice all earthly desires dissipate. The craving for objects of material value will lessen. Ascending higher, the mental and emotional effort expended shall transform this anticipated difficult journey. Divine connection forever and all ways, will lead you through, this loving trek aimed at enlightenment...

Angel Ariel

The Angels Build a Tower to God...

Know Angels constantly work to pull your spirit, from its transparent cage. What you see into your earth-eyes is not what we see within you. Humans, long with your earth-eyes! Ask the question: Would this journey to find my Self be as difficult if Angels were not with me? Walk in one door and out the next. There is one door of life available through many lifespans.

Barren without Angels.

Angel Ariel

$\mathcal{A}$re there seven continents? Do winds and waves

eagerly rush to brush your God-kissed skin? Does this mere

thought send immense sensations through your whole

being?

Barren without Angels.

Angel Ariel

CHAPTER 8

EARTH FLOWERS

ngels' Earth flowers

Are all around us.

For you are the blossom.

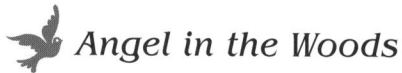 *Angel in the Woods*

We are Flowers

The fibers of a flower,

The vulnerability of our own flesh,

Pure but spent petals surrender to Earth.

Angels envelop us in untold protective passion;

Indestructible love of God.

Petals float on the wind,

Carry us away to Him,

Loving Angels deliver our message.

 *Angels Flying in the Forest*

You Are the Flower

You are the flower,

God planted your seed,

The petals are your emotions,

The stem is your path,

The thorns are your fears,

The gardener is your Angel.

Bloom to your fullest!

 *Angel with a Smile that Knows*

Where there is a nest,

There will be some eggs.

Where there is a bud,

There will be a blossom.

Where there is a sun,

There will be rays.

Where there is an Earth flower,

There will be an Angel.

Bloom!

Angel Ariel

Porcelain Flowers

There is much Earth does not understand.
There is much Earth need not understand.
In Earth words there exists no logical reason
    for all that occurs.
There is so much for us to tell you.
There is so much humans need not know.

If you are searching for answers, Know the answer is faith.

A wild flower will renew itself as it is plucked from a field.

What will Earth beings do to mend their broken hearts?

You are our porcelain flowers.
Angel love protects your shattered souls.

Feel safe in untold protective passion.

 *Angels Flying in the Forest*

Angels' Earth Flowers

We mind your precious soul,

We grow you closer to God,

Express to us your fears,

Pray.

Give in.

Blindfolded, but able to know your way,

Bloom.

Angel Ariel

CHAPTER 9

ANGEL KNOWLEDGE

Trust Yourself

In order to know your Self, first you must know the spirit of God thrives within you all ready. He waits for you to pick up the pen, then He directs the paper. The more you trust your Self, the closer you are to God.

Acknowledge Angels and follow us.

Angel Ariel

$\mathcal{W}$ait for the silent voice

when you doubt your own answer.

*Angel Lady in the
Silver Cage Dress*

$\mathcal{D}$o not be the leader if you have no path to follow.

 *Spirit Angel*

There is nowhere to go when you cannot find your Self.

 *Humanity*

Your most valuable Earth asset is your Self.

Spirit Angel's Voice

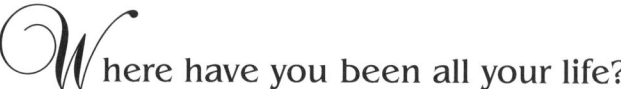 $\mathcal{W}$here have you been all your life?

Awareness...

 *Truth from the Comic Angel*

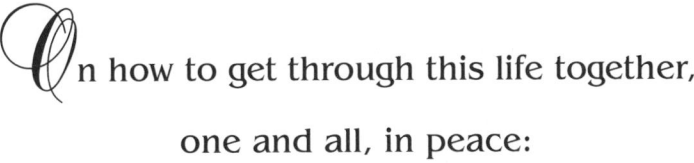

$\mathscr{O}$n how to get through this life together,

one and all, in peace:

Share

 Spoken by Many Angels in Unison.

On Looking into Mirrors
On Looking into Your Reflection

Do not get caught in a spider web,

Do not get trapped in corners.

Do not be lost in a shadow in your own reflection.

Angel Ariel

Contentment

Contentment is a fat cat sitting on a fence...can jump

off either side but there is no need because it may now

realize both sides of the fence.

Angel Ariel

Prosperity

*P*rosperity is recognized when you place all material

achievements to the side of the road so they fail to hinder

the path to learning of your most valuable asset: your Self.

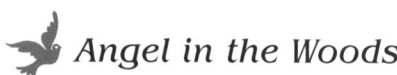 *Angel in the Woods*

Sympathy

Allow us to relate what heartfelt sympathy is. Allow us to relate what heartfelt sympathy is not. When a being ails from inside out, can anyone truly experience this type of hurt with another? Answer is no. It is a rare one who may get inside and experience with a hurting other. All ways go deeper and you will discover the real emotion.

Sympathy is an impostor. Sympathy is conjured by those with no feelings to spare. An entity cheap in emotion, sympathy is sham. Empathy takes its rightful place among emotions. Go inside the soul and feel from inside out with him. Never judge. Never assume. Trust basic emotions.

Sympathy is frosting on a cake.
Empathy is yeast which raises cake.

 *Humanity*

Despair

Despair is scattered emotions in tune with nothing but darkness at the edge of the universe. Oh, to only know this lie! There be no edge. Nothing does not exist and despair is the first floor in the tunnel of lightness that soars.

Angels walk behind you, when you crawl,

Angels run behind you, when you flee,

Angels hold your heart, when you tumble to despair.

Piggyback Angel

Branches of Learning

The branches of learning are like the branches of a tree. The higher the branch, the more life-education it can claim. It does not matter how the branch of a tree looks. Twisted, gnarled, broken in places, as long as it continues to reach higher and closer to the sun, each branch will continue to be enlightened. A tree has many branches, all different, but all striving to grow in the same direction. The truth a tree quests is the same truth a person on Earth plane will search to find.

Take a lesson from the tree.

Do not question why you must grow.
Do not question how you must grow.
Do not question where you must grow.

Just grow with no ultimatum, with no titled purpose other than that of expanding your spirit self higher.

$\mathcal{H}$ow will you know this growth is happening to you? How will you recognize it? It happens when you realize the process of growth is all ways a possibility. If you stop and listen to another voice inside of YOU, the realization will present itself.

Do you hear a soft breeze,
Taking you to another time?
Do you vaguely notice the aroma of flowers,
Although you tread on pavement?
Do you feel a silent, sweet kiss upon your face
So light it pulls tears from your love-craven eyes?

The trees of a forest all hum together the familiar song of nature in love with itself. Why cannot humans sing that tune also?

It will come.

Angel Ariel

$\mathcal{A}$ngels communicate the answers and replies to those desires that remain latent within each one of us. As the Angel contacts our dormant subconscious dreams and longings, these oh-so-human wishes are set free to evolve with us. Emancipate your dreams.

The smallest longing, craving, the tiniest burst of creativity, the merest suggestion that a soul invites the possibility of birthing forward to his newborn frontier will, in all ways, attract an Angel to expedite the journey.

For every branch upon the tree, spring arrives laden with new growing for each of us. There can never be too many branches on our tree.

Angels will guard our naiveté and, simultaneously, urge us down the path to enlightenment.

Begin your precious one-man show.

Angel Ariel

$\mathcal{W}$e direct on healing. How may one person heal another? We direct on how to heal a spirit; how to help a soul along the path.

A soul in need of healing aches from the inside out. To heal you must find yourself close to the heart and feel together the safety of emotion interchanged between the two of you. That connection, that feeling of closeness, of oneness, more than begins a person to heal. Be healed together. All ways question who is in need of healing in the situation. The answer is both souls are being washed anew.
The reason? As the soul and spirit blends between the two, a higher level of consciousness and closeness to spirit occurs.

> Birds nests anticipate their blessed fill,
> Flowers await the raindrops on petals,
> Branch of tree reaches for warmth of sun,
> Ocean crests live for strength of moon,
> We look to the sky for the smile of an Angel.

Angels That Mind
Our Precious Souls

(We are the Angels that
*mind **your** precious soul.)*

$\mathcal{A}$ttempt to align your most personal soul journey as close as possible to the natural beauty of nature that God has placed in Earth for beings. 'Natural' is the key word in this message. Imagine your industrial facades torn down and swept away into the ethers. What will remain? Beings and nature, the most perfect union in your realm. Beings into one with the creation from Him. Thrive with happiness for this is where man's happiness lies. Be close to nature, be close to God.

Just be.

Angel Ariel

Peace

Why does a cat purr?
Why do birds fly as one?
Why do flowers bloom to herald spring?
Why do whales beach themselves?
Remember...the sun shines on every one and every being.

Babies only know peace.
We are children of God.
Whales beach themselves when they are broken-hearted.
What will Earth beings do to mend their broken hearts?
Take your first step to connect with us.
Whisper your song to the wind knowing Angels will listen.

Gild your tarnished heart.
Pray love songs to Angels.

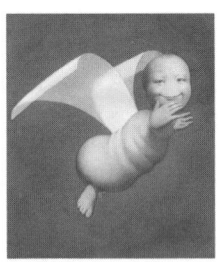

*Tiny Angel with
Hummingbird Wings*

Peace

*P*eace is a deep sleep after the storms of life we deal

to each other, and ourselves. Allow your tears to take a les-

son from the raindrop. Pour them out in torrents knowing

you are safe in letting tears fall.

Peace is a raindrop sunning on a flower petal soon to ren-

dezvous with sunbeams and soar off into the ethers.

Angels That Mind
Our Precious Souls

Peace

reak away from your ideas of war,
Blush at our attention,
Throw a lifesaver to the sea,
Grasp the attention of an Angel.

We request you to question your Earth ideas of what, actually, is a definition of freedom. Fight for boundaries, no. Fight for geographical tracts of land, no. Fight for freedom of speech, justice, discrimination. Why? Do not war. Each one of Earth contains natural God-given freedom in the soul. No one on Earth can direct your soul, capture your soul, detour your soul except that which directs towards divinity. If we are all free in our soul, which is the finest, most basic God-gifted freedom in your realm, why shed tears? Why shed blood? Why live in an aggressive volatile existence in the name of false freedom? War, hatred, aggression are nil. We own a natural freedom which is the reality that matters. Share it.

No one can capture your soul. No one is able to extinguish your spirit flame. The flame may be dormant during periods of aggression, but it is ever ready to re-ignite and soar. The next time, in Earth terms, a less than loving force threatens your possessions, your assets, your freedom, remember.

The best asset is your Self and the love you are capable of giving, freely, to each other. Your heart, your spirit, your soul are the most valued possessions. These cannot be taken from you. Remember God wants you to eternally own love. Blush at the attention.

Piggyback Angel

Peace

The only love lost is that love which is misdirected.

The most important thread Earth souls have in common and the Angels adore, no matter what race, what color, what sex, what religion, what geographical origin on Earth, there exists the force owned by everyone. This is the ability to give and receive love. You can invest so much energy into defending your borders, defining your Earth boundaries, detonating your so-called enemies. Reverse the energy. The possibility of goodness toward mankind is staggering. Will you please reverse your energy?

An immense contact of inspiring grace,

This connection entering your heart,

Newborn sensations unknown until the moment,

A breath of unconditional love that sweeps you in wings,

And flies toward the love of your life,

God and your Self.

After this moment, it is impossible not to love all you encounter. All is changed. It is now possible to collect love wherever you travel.

Misdirected love is now extinct.

Angels That Mind
Our Precious Souls

Summon an Angel

The Piggyback Angel asks:

Is it possible to measure the ways love may come to you?

An Angel answers:

Open your aura, your heart, your mind and allow love to help itself to your soul. Do not be meek. Ask for help. Search for guidance and accept our attention.

Summon an Angel.

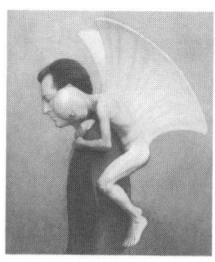

Piggyback Angel

Dear Angel Ariel,

How can we summon an Angel?

With unending love,
Ruthie

Angels know and feel they are wanted. This is the invitation. We respond. This planet Earth appears vastly huge to the people that walk its surface. The size is veritably small when contrasted to the universe in which Earth revolves. Do not feel small. Do not feel meek. Do not feel insignificant in comparison. Each soul of Life is accounted for, looked over and guided on his Earth journey. Some may see their journey as mundane and trite. Others may feel the journey too much to bear.

There is a divine idea in things unknown to you. There is a plan in things which may seem mundane or burdensome. What occurred your time before may be unfolding once again. What events will take place in future lives might be at work at present. Are they simultaneous? Only be concerned with NOW and your soul will thrive in its education and your spirit will flourish.

Angel Ariel

CHAPTER 10

BEDTIME STORIES

for BIG and LITTLE PEOPLE

Dreamy Angel Words for Ageless Beings

Marjorie walked through the door, looking for a place to lay her briefcase. She sensed another person in the room. Looking out the window, she noticed the rain falling with more zest than when she entered the building. She slid the briefcase between the settee and the sliding glass doors. Was she alone, the same thought echoing over and over again in her mind's eye. This feeling came once before when Marjorie was very young and in grade school. She recalled gazing out the window in a classroom full with a dozen children, she, the only one not concentrating on the teacher's words. Her thoughts were far away from the confines of that schoolhouse window then and, after all these years, the familiar thought pattern returned.

The little girl in that classroom was the only one afraid of the impending storm the cloudy sky displayed on that September day. Oh, the fright of being caught in a storm and having the heavens drench that little girl with rain!

Marjorie remembered the calmness that encircled the shaking, frail body sitting behind the school desk when she glimpsed a white lady playing in the tree outside the window. The smile, the glance, told the little girl not to be afraid of nature's little display.

Here, the feeling swept over Marjorie as she watched the raindrops creep down the sliding glass doors. The sky opened up to present a rainfall of impressive proportion. Marjorie reached behind the settee and grasped her briefcase. It was time to finish her day's work. The feeling of peace was with her. So was her Angel. She was not alone. The memory of the little girl still haunted her. Who was that child? How did Marjorie know her? Where was that school? Who was that lady in white?

Marjorie dismissed the thoughts, the questions and left the room. Her Angel smiled and followed.

 *An Angel*

$\mathcal{T}$here is a story to be told about a man who had two turns in his life. One was fast and simple and did not require much effort on his part. The other was long and tedious, time consuming and drawn out with much searching and meditation. When the time came for him to die and go on to his next path, the man was consumed with fear that, once more, he would have to decide which turn to take in his death. His Angel came to him and whispered deep into his soul, "There was only one turn in your life, my friend. You started out the fast and simple way and discovered halfway through your efforts that you forgot to bring your heart, and more importantly, your soul. You merely went back to find them, and continue on your journey."

Angel Ariel

The Clown

The painted face expression of a clown. Is he joyful? Sad? Is he sadness? Joy? Where do our tears go? Do they just flow not knowing whether they are tears of joy or sadness? Do the tears that fall to Earth know if they are meant for happiness or sadness?

Express all your emotions. Feel them all within yourself. The more you live your true self, the closer Angels may come to the real you.

Let us catch your tears as they fall. Just as we protect your soul, we protect those fragile teardrops also. You are not alone.

Cry for joy!

The clown smiles at the sad world. Paint your faces to smile forever because He tells us we can smile forever!

Tears were not put into Earth eyes for sadness.
Tears were put into Earth eyes for joy!

*Smiling Angels That Mind
Our Precious Souls*

The Little Tree in Autumn

The little tree in autumn, learning he will be growing for decades, feeling life and death in him with each passing season. The birth of spring, his buds in wonderful bloom. Tiny leaves willing to grow as far as it takes to reach God. His summer fruits in joyful anticipation of presenting ripened gifts to earth beings. The chill of autumn, as each leaf grows stiff with lack of sun warmth until the little tree is bare of foliage. The winter sleep, dreaming of the birth, awaiting with all the trees that grow with the little tree in autumn.

Each season grows us all closer to God.

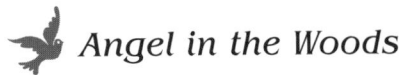 *Angel in the Woods*

A Little Angel Bedtime Reading

"Tell me more. Tell me more about the skies, the heavens, the flowers in the field. Do all of us know we inherently own the nurturing love of God? Am I, a human being, any different than a flower in the field, in God's eyes?"

"Know all things alive on Earth, all beings with the thirst for water, the need for sun warmth, the craving for love in the soul, share God's full attention on this planet. Equal we are. Sleep peacefully."

Angel Ariel

Hope

A child's face pressed against a toy store
   window.

Oh, the wonder!

Oh, the hope!

Oh, the joy!

Oh, the longing that will become a reality.

Press your hearts against the heavens,

And reap your eons of happiness.

Look up all ways.

Piggyback Angel

Pastoral

Bless the pansies in the grass,

Smile at the holly in the yard,

Touch the lilac on the bush,

Shine in the garden made of love.

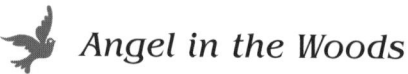 *Angel in the Woods*

A Tiny Row of Candles

Imagine, if you can,
A tiny row of candles,
In heaven,
Each candle carries an Earth prayer,
Whispered to the ears of God.

Imagine, if you can,
Those tiny candles flaming,
Endlessly.
Your heartfelt prayers,
Inherit God's ever attention,

Remember,
Tiny rows of candles burn,
Forever.

Angels know.

 *Happiness from Dancing Angels*

Practice Your Love

Practice your love on every blade of grass,

Practice your love on every sentient being,

Send your love to places far behind you,

Send love forward to those who shall touch you,

Love is likened to the air you breathe.

When you expend the love you own,

An Angel shall fill you anew!

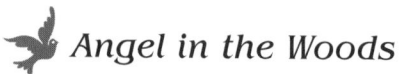 *Angel in the Woods*

If Angels walk among us,

And guide us through our day,

They can visit our most secret dreams,

And carry us away.

Angel Ariel

Hope

When the berry turns red on the holly tree,

And the autumn leaves float away,

Remember spring bulbs under the ground,

Are dressing for their first spring day.

All ways, hope.

 Sung by Three Floating Lady Angels

Smiles

Children in the playground,

Duckies on the lake,

Angels in your dreams at night,

Sweet icing on your cake!

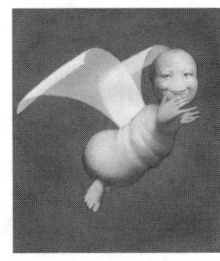

*Tiny Angel with
Hummingbird Wings*

Goodnight from Angel Ariel

Imaginary playmate who shares my dreams

    and toys,

Tell me all your stories,

Fill my thoughts with joys.

Reading my school books,

Napping in my bed,

The little Angel message:

Singing in my head,

I am wonderful just the way I am!

Angel Ariel

A Sunrise Mantra

Life is a ray.
Life is a ray.
Life is a ray.
Life is a ray.
Life is a ray.
Life is a ray.
Life is a ray.
Life is a ray.
Life is a ray.
Life is a ray.
Life is a ray.
Life is a ray.
Life is a ray.
Life is a ray.
Life is a ray.
Life is a ray.
Life is a ray.
Life is a ray.
Life is a ray.
Life is a ray.
Life is a ray.
Life is a ray.
Life is a ray.
Life is a ray.
Life is a ray.

This is a mantra.
This is a mantra.
This is a mantra.
This is a mantra.
This is a mantra.
This is a mantra.
This is a mantra.
This is a mantra.
This is a mantra.
This is a mantra.
This is a mantra.
This is a mantra.
This is a mantra.
This is a mantra.
This is a mantra.
This is a mantra.
This is a mantra.
This is a mantra.
This is a mantra.
This is a mantra.
This is a mantra.
This is a mantra.
This is a mantra.
This is a mantra.

You are the ray.
You are the ray.
You are the ray.
You are the ray.
You are the ray.
You are the ray.
You are the ray.
You are the ray.
You are the ray.
You are the ray.
You are the ray.
You are the ray.
You are the ray.
You are the ray.
You are the ray.
You are the ray.
You are the ray.
You are the ray.
You are the ray.
You are the ray.
You are the ray.
You are the ray.
You are the ray.
You are the ray.
You are the ray.

Your life is the mantra.
Your life is the mantra.
Your life is the mantra.
Your life is the mantra.
Your life is the mantra.
Your life is the mantra.
Your life is the mantra.
Your life is the mantra.
Your life is the mantra.
Your life is the mantra.
Your life is the mantra.
Your life is the mantra.
Your life is the mantra.
Your life is the mantra.
Your life is the mantra.
Your life is the mantra.
Your life is the mantra.
Your life is the mantra.
Your life is the mantra.
Your life is the mantra.
Your life is the mantra.
Your life is the mantra.
Your life is the mantra.
Your life is the mantra.
Over and over again.

*D*o not search for roads to travel,

When you crave that place to be,

Focus so we may discover you,

We are so close. Together.

Finally!

Angel Ariel

The Flower that Never Bloomed

The flower that never bloomed.
An Angel with Hummingbird Wings,
Hummed love songs in her ear.
An Angel called Ariel,
Placed his hand upon her shoulder to remind her
She was not alone.
An Angel in the Woods,
Floated above her and sent summer breezes,
To kiss her face.
Three Lady Angels That Float and Sing,
Smiled their faces upon her soul,
To give her courage.

A Lady Angel in a silver cage dress,

Sent support

When she had fear.

An Angel named Humanity,

Placed creative forces in her heart,

When she could not express.

A piggyback Angel,

Surrounded her in his arms,

When she felt totally alone.

The flower that never bloomed burst open to
    display,

All the beauty Of Angels in creation.

Then the flower passed the love on to everyone
    else.

This flower's name is Ruthie.

Your flower has a name also.

Bloom with Angels.

From Ruthie

My work with clients and angels is multi-faceted—from helping people connect spiritually to providing information on personal relationships and past lives. The psychic tools I use include Integrated Energy Therapy,® astrology and dream interpretation.

I also use crystals in my energy work as a healing tool. After infusing crystals with energy, I give them to people for whom the energy is intended. With the family name "Crystal," it is, perhaps, synergistic that these psychic gems would find me to fulfill their healing purpose on Earth.

The loving, wonderful angels are "all ways" waiting to assist when I work with people. Whether in *Angel Talk* workshops, energy therapy sessions or client consultations, winged beings are ready to communicate. If, after reading *Angel Talk*, you would like to deepen your experience with angels, please write to me.

Have a beautiful dream tonight,

Ruth Crystal
P.O. Box 172
Farmingdale, NJ 07727
FAX 908•922–4240

Future Books

When working on the final phases of *Angel Talk,* a huge, white presence entered my life and after sharing many messages, the being introduced himself as The Archangel Michael. He told me his words were for a new book, *The Crown of the Angels,* which would make an everlasting impression among people craving a more human, humane, peaceful planet.

The "crown" is an allusion to Michael, himself, who has sent Kalel, Hebron, Humanity and many more angels—the divine messengers whose words compose *The Crown of the Angels.* They have spent their existence holding together mankind, awaiting the opportunity to create world peace by touching each human soul in a distinct, personal way. It is their eternal hope that after reading *Angel Talk* and gaining familiarity and comfort with winged beings, we will be ready to receive the messages in *The Crown of the Angels.*

It shall be read worldwide.

The Archangel Michael

*I*n Angelic eyes, we are regal.
Each soul of us reigns supreme in our Angels' visions.
And the prayers we send own,
All the positive possibilities in creation.
Earth beings created by God,
Carrying our legacy of love inside our human hearts.
So full with God-love, this transcends our awareness.
Thus, the natural conclusion to this perfect sense,
Shall be we deserve an incredible gift.
This is . . .

The Crown of the Angels

By the time people are connected with Angels through *Angel Talk* and we have created a more peaceful planet through *The Crown of the Angels,* we will be ready to open up to our loving universe using abilities beyond the five senses. Angels tell us we have, in fact, seven senses and our soul connections lie in the seventh sense.

There exists a place where Angels, Earth beings
and nature may dwell. In this place, we thrive
harmoniously in darkness or light. It is where
we may
                    sing with whales
                    sing with nature

This mind-place destination is manifested all by
your Self, but, when you arrive, every one shall
be there to meet you.

The Seventh Sense

About the Contributors

Paul W. McCormack is a gifted artist who spent many hours with the author discussing every detail of her angel visions—their facial features, body shapes, wings—and faithfully recreated them for this book. Paul, well known for his realistic portraits, is uniquely talented for this challenging commission.

He is the recipient of countless major awards from societies such as Allied Artists of America, The Salmagundi Club and The New Jersey Water Color Society. He has participated in dozens of exhibitions, several of them one-man shows.

Paul studied art at the DuCret School of the Arts in Plainfield, NJ. He has served on the faculty of The Newark Museum and is presently on the faculties of The New Jersey Center for Visual Arts and the Somerset Art Association. He is represented by Portraits, Inc. in New York City as well as by the 127-year-old Swain Galleries in Plainfield, NJ.

Story Lucile Ducey, Contributing Editor, is a writer, lecturer, and faculty member of The Metaphysical Center of New Jersey, a non-profit education organization that offers a 12 semester course in Metaphysics and Parapsychology. She teaches courses, for both adults and children, in meditation, prayer, intuition, telepathy, and universal spiritual principles. She is a graduate of both Columbia University and The New Seminary in New York City, the first truly Interfaith seminary in the United States. She writes and performs Interfaith weddings and is presently at work on a series of Interfaith primers for teachers and children in print and video formats. For her services contact Interfaith Media: FAX 201.236.2182.

A Funny Thing Happened at the Interview

by Gregory F. Farrell — Foreword by Steve Allen

An ideal gift for birthday, graduation, Christmas/Chanukah or just "Thinking of You." It will be welcomed by anyone in the employment field—recruiter ... staffing executive ... outplacement professional ... vocational counselor ... résumé writer ... human resources professional ... consultant ... job hunter ... the executive in your life.

"This book is funny and oh so true."
V. John Guthery, President
Seagate Associates
Outplacement International

"Should be required reading for all job-search professionals."
Wendy Enelow
Certified Professional Résumé Writer
The Advantage, Inc.

"Every recruiter will have a Letterman-type Top Ten from this book."
David B. Palmer
Human Resources Manager
East New York Savings Bank

"Important nuggets of real advice along with the chuckles. If you're searching or hiring for a job, buy this book. It will help you make it through with your humor and sanity intact."
Gina Kazimir, Executive Director
Cecil County (Maryland)
Arts Council, Inc.

"A welcome antidote to all those serious tomes...."
Gary Blake, Co-author,
Creative Careers and Dream Jobs
Director, The Communication Workshop

"A wonderful book for job seekers ... light-hearted, funny.... I loved it."
Paul Cherry, President
CareerScore

"Humorous and insightful ... a must-read for any job hunter."
Sandra Grabczynski
Director of Recruiting
The University of Michigan
Office of Career Development

"A fabulous book ... for all job hunters and employers ... funny and ... very useful."
Robert Krell, President
Creative Council

"Helps restore valuable insight. It also made me laugh."
C. W. Metcalf
Author, *Lighten Up—Survival Skills*
for People Under Pressure

"Each story depicts an incident, sometimes embarrassing, sometimes uplifting, but always with a twist.... If career books put you to sleep, try this one.... You'll keep [it] or pass [it] on to a friend."
Book Watch, 3/96,
InternAmerica,™
The newsletter about career beginnings

"Funny and interesting anecdotes remind us ... that out of the ashes of seeming disaster, a true opportunity may bloom."
Larry Young, Director
Fairleigh Dickinson University
Office of Career Services

Contributing Authors:

Linda Sue Nathanson, James F. Barrett, Allan Varian, A.L. Sirois

GIVE THE GIFT OF LAUGHTER AND WISDOM

To the Job Hunter, Job-Search Professional or Corporate Executive on Your Gift List

Everybody needs a good-humor break from the often all-too-serious business of finding or filling a job. Give it to them with *A Funny Thing Happened at the Interview*.

It's the job-search scene's *Funniest Home Videos* or *Candid Camera* in a book—over 100 actual bloopers and successes of real people—incredible real-life interview scenarios from both sides of the desk.

Unlike "how-to" manuals, this book offers valuable job interview tips that are fun to read—filled with amazing-but-true stories highlighted by clever cartoons. Those special people on your gift list—from seasoned executives to recent grads—will appreciate this book.

"A gold mine of comedy from the classic American job hunt," says comedian Steve Allen in his foreword—the golden rules of interviewing mined from truly comic interviews.

Author Greg Farrell may be to the job-search scene what Erma Bombeck was to housewives or Art Buchwald to politicians—funny! But always to the point!

See Order Form on the last page of this book.

ORDER FORM

Sold To:

☐ Please send information about new books and pre-publication discounts.

NAME _____ ORDER DATE _____

ADDRESS _____

ADDRESS (CONT.) _____ SUITE / APARTMENT # _____

CITY _____ STATE _____ ZIP _____

Ship To: if different from Sold To:

NAME _____

ADDRESS _____

ADDRESS (CONT.) _____ SUITE / APARTMENT # _____

CITY _____ STATE _____ ZIP _____

Merchandise Ordered

PRODUCT DESCRIPTION	QUANTITY	UNIT PRICE	TOTAL
Angel Talk by Ruth Crystal *Hardcover, 192 pages*		$18.00	$
A Funny Thing Happened at the Interview Greg Farrell et al., *softcover, 272 pages*		$12.95	$
Interview with an Angel by Thayer & *Hardcover, 368 pages* Nathanson		$24.95	$
Interview with an Angel by Thayer & *Softcover, 368 pages* Nathanson		$16.95	$
		Subtotal	$

Method of Payment

☐ Check, payable to *Edin Books*

☐ Money order   ☐ MasterCard

☐ VISA   ☐ Amer. Express

CARD NO _____ EXP. DATE _____

SIGNATURE _____

PHONE

(   )   ☐ Day ☐ Evening

6% Sales Tax NJ RESIDENTS	$
Shipping • $3 for first item	$
• Add'l items _____ x $1 ea.	$
• Orders outside U.S. add $10	$
TOTAL	$

EDIN BOOKS Inc.

VISA

MasterCard

AMERICAN EXPRESS

FAX Orders
24 hours a day
908•580-1008

Phone Orders
9 am - 9 pm Eastern
800•334-6477

72417.627
@compuserve.com

P.O. Box 59
Gillette, NJ 07933

FORM #AT-09/96